What is phonics?

Phonics helps children learn to read and write by teaching them the letter sounds (known as phonemes), rather than the letter names, e.g. the sound that 'c' makes rather than its alphabetic name. They then learn how to blend the sounds: the process of saying the sounds in a word or 'sounding out' and then blending them together to make the word, for example c – a – t = cat. Once the phonemes and the skill of blending are learnt, children can tackle reading any phonetically decodable word they come across, even ones they don't know, with confidence and success.

However, there are of course many words in the English language that aren't phonetically decodable, e.g. if a child gets stuck on 'the' it doesn't help if they sound it out and blend it. We call these 'tricky words' and they are just taught as words that are so 'tricky' that children have to learn to recognise them by sight.

How do phonic readers work?

Phonic reading books are written especially for children who are beginning to learn phonics at nursery or school, and support any programme being used by providing plenty of practice as children develop the skills of decoding and blending. By targeting specific phonemes and tricky words, increasing in difficulty, they ensure systematic progression with reading.

Because phonic readers are primarily decodable – aside from the target tricky words which need to be learnt, children should be able to read the books with real assurance and accomplishment.

Big Cat phonic readers:
Pond Food

In Big Cat phonic readers the specific phonemes and tricky words being focussed on are highlighted here in these notes, so that you can be clear about what your child's learning and what they need to practise.

While reading at home together, there are all sorts of fun additional games you can play to help your child practise those phonemes and tricky words, which can be a nice way to familiarise yourselves with them before reading, or remind you of them after you've finished. In *Pond Food*, for example:

- the focus phonemes are sh (fish), ee (weeds), ai (snails), ck (quack), x (fox). Why not write them down and encourage your child to practise saying the sounds as you point to them in a random order. This is called 'Speed Sounds' and as you get faster and faster with your pointing, it encourages your child to say them as quickly as possible. You can try reversing the roles, so that you have a practice too!

- the tricky words are 'the', 'are' and 'no' . You can play 'Hide and Seek' by asking your child to close their eyes and count to 10, while you write each word on a piece of paper, hiding them somewhere in the room you're in or the garden for your child to find. As they find each one, they should try reading and spelling the word out.

Reading together

- Look at the front cover of *Pond Food* and talk about what you can see.

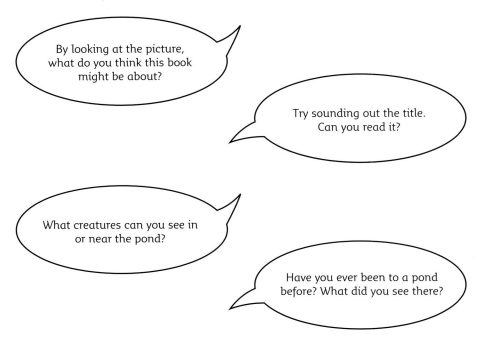

By looking at the picture, what do you think this book might be about?

Try sounding out the title. Can you read it?

What creatures can you see in or near the pond?

Have you ever been to a pond before? What did you see there?

- Enjoy reading *Pond Food* together, noticing the focus phonemes (sh, ee, ai, ck, x) and tricky words (the, are, no). It's useful to point to each word as your child reads, and encouraging to give them lots of praise as they go.

- If your child gets stuck on a word, and it's phonetically decodable, encourage them to sound it out. You can practise blending by saying the sounds aloud a few times, getting quicker and quicker. If they still can't read it, tell them the word and move on.

Talking about the book

- Use the picture on pp18–19 to talk about the food chain: which creature eats which food, and what each creature does.

- Practise the focus phonemes from *Pond Food* by asking your child to tell you which sound, for example, the word 'splash' ends with, or how they'd sound out some of the key words, for example, 'fox' and 'snails'.

Pond Food

Written by John Townsend
Illustrated by Pamela Anzalotti

Collins

The pond has a lot of
food in it.

Weeds are in
the pond.

Snails are in the pond.

Snails feed on the weeds.

Fish swim in the pond.

Fish feed on the snails.

Frogs hop and plop in
the pond.

12

Frogs feed on the fish.

Ducks quack and splash on the pond.

Ducks feed on the frogs.

A fox looks for food at
the pond.

The pond has no food
for the fox today.

The pond

weed

snail

fish

frog

fox

duck

19

Getting creative

- Have some fun with your child by playing a game of 'Phoneme Detectives', where they look through the book and write down all the words that contain one of the focus phonemes. Which phoneme is in the most words? Can they think of anymore words?

- To practise the tricky words from *Pond Food*, try writing them down on pieces of paper and putting each one on a separate stair of your staircase. Your child can then try reading them as they go up and down the stairs!

- If your child's enjoyed reading *Pond Food*, why not see if they'd like to make their own pond picture, by drawing all the creatures in the pond, cutting them out and sticking them on to a tin-foil 'pond'. They could then research other pond animals, and label them all.

Other books at Level 1:

Fiction	Non-fiction
Sam and the Nut — Sheryl Webster, Giuditta Gaviraghi	Got It! — Charlotte Guillain, Lee Honor Roberts
Ant and Snail — Paul Shipton, Jon Stuart	Pet Cat, Big Cat — Alison Hawes
We Are Not Fond of Rat! — Emma Chichester Clark	Pond Food — John Townsend, Pamela Anzalotti

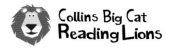

Collins Big Cat
Reading Lions

Published by Collins
An imprint of HarperCollins*Publishers*
1 London Bridge Street
London
SE1 9GF

© HarperCollins*Publishers* 2011
This edition was published in 2015.

Author: John Townsend

British Library Cataloguing in Publication Data
A catalogue record for this publication is available from the British Library.

Illustrator: Pamela Anzalotti
Designer: Rachel Clark
Parent notes authors: Sue Reed and Liz Webster

Printed and bound by RR Donnelley APS

www.collins.co.uk/parents